# WHAT EVERY STUDENT SHOULD KNOW ABOUT CITING SOURCES WITH APA DOCUMENTATION

**Chalon E. Anderson**
*University of Central Oklahoma*

**Amy T. Carrell**
*University of Central Oklahoma*

**Jimmy L. Widdifield, Jr.**
*Contributing Author*

PEARSON

Boston   New York   San Francisco
Mexico City   Montreal   Toronto   London   Madrid   Munich   Paris
Hong Kong   Singapore   Tokyo   Cape Town   Sydney

Series Editor: Stephen Frail
Series Editorial Assistant: Allison Rowland
Executive Marketing Manager, Psychology: Karen Natale
Production Editor: Won McIntosh
Editorial Production Service: WestWords, Inc.
Composition Buyer: Linda Cox
Manufacturing Buyer: JoAnne Sweeney
Electronic Composition: WestWords, Inc.
Cover Administrator: Elena Sidorova

For related titles and support materials, visit our online catalog at www.ablongman.com.

Between the time website information is gathered and then published, it is not unusual for
some sites to have closed. Also, the transcription of URLs can result in typographical errors.
The publisher would appreciate notification where these errors occur so that they may be
corrected in subsequent editions.

Anderson, Chalon.
  What every student should know about citing sources with APA documentation /
Chalon E. Anderson, Amy T. Carrell, Jimmy L. Widdifield, Jr. -- 1st ed.
    p. cm.
Includes bibliographical references.
  ISBN 0-205-49923-6
  1. Psychology--Authorship--Handbooks, manuals, etc. 2. Social
sciences--Authorship--Handbooks, manuals, etc. 3. Report writing--Handbooks,
manuals, etc. I. Carrell, Amy. II. Widdifield, Jimmy L. III. Title

BF76.7A55 2006
808'.06615--dc22

                                                                2006042998

Printed in the United States of America

10          CRS   10  09  08

# CONTENTS

# PREFACE

One component common to all educational endeavors is the ability to express ideas, research, and stories in a format that can be understood. Many students have come to realize that this means more than putting lines on a page. In the social sciences, a formal writing format is required. The writing format that has been accepted as the standard in the social sciences is from the American Psychological Association (APA).

Many students dread the inference and imposition of any writing format but eventually understand the need for consistency in formal writing. This guide, which we have written to be "user friendly," is meant to assist students in their writing. We believe that this guide will also be useful to faculty instructing students in the use of the APA format, but we also believe that the guide can stand alone for use by students not enrolled in a research-writing course. Finally, we have included a manuscript that has been formatted in APA style.

It is our hope that this guide will help ease the worries of correct citations and proper referencing and enable you to focus on the research and writing of excellent papers.

*Chalon E. Anderson*
*Amy Carrell*
*Jimmy L. Widdifield, Jr.*

# 1

# THE BASICS: APA RULES

The APA has determined that manuscripts written using this format should follow specific guidelines. The basic essentials of APA follow:

- The manuscript should be on white bond paper, 8 1/2 by 11 inches. Pages should be printed on only one side of the paper.
- Standard margins are 1 inch on all four sides.
- The manuscript is double-spaced.
- Use 12-point Times New Roman or Courier font.
- The pages of the manuscript should appear in the following sequence: title page, abstract, text pages (introduction, methods, results, and discussion), references, appendixes, notes, tables, figure captions, and figures (the figures appear on separate pages, one per page).
- All pages are numbered, beginning with the title page, in the right upper corner, five spaces after the last word of the header, which is 1/2 inch from the top edge and 1 inch from the right edge of the paper.
- The abstract starts the second page of the paper. The word *Abstract* is typed and centered 1 inch from the top of the page, on page 2.
- The abstract should not exceed 960 characters (approximately 120 words), including punctuation and spaces.

- The actual text of the manuscript begins on page 3. The title of the manuscript appears in sentence case, centered at the top of the page.
- Use words to spell out numbers one through nine and Arabic numerals to express numbers starting at 10 and continuing forward.
- When beginning a sentence, spell out the number regardless of the value.
- If two numbers are grouped for comparison, use Arabic numerals regardless of the numbers' values.
- Use Arabic numerals to express exact measurements.
- The primary headings (i.e., Abstract, Introduction, Methods, Results, and Discussion) should be continuous and should not purposely start a new page. EXCEPTION: Begin a new page for the references and appendix. The word *References* should be typed in sentence case and centered at the top of the page, as should the word *Appendix*.
- The second line of each reference is indented five spaces, or 1/2 inch.
- The appendix follows the reference page. The word *Appendix* appears typed in sentence case, centered 1 inch from the top of the page. If there is more than one appendix, use capital letters (beginning with *A*) to identify each appendix (e.g., Appendix A, Appendix B, etc.).
- Indent the first line of text in the appendix five spaces, or 1/2 inch.
- If tables are included in the appendix, their titles must reflect the fact that they are part of the appendix (e.g., Appendix Table A1).
- If figures are to be added to the appendix, begin by identifying them by Figure 1, Figure 2, etc.
- All notes, such as author, copyright, and table notes, should begin on a separate page following the appendixes. The title *Notes* is centered on the page in sentence case.
- All tables follow the appendixes, and each table appears on a separate page.

- Tables and figures are numbered sequentially but separately; that is, there will be Table 1 and Figure 1.
- All basic formatting rules apply to tables.
- When introducing a table or figure in the appendix, use the words *Table* and *Figure,* with their numerical correspondence. This text should be left justified.
- The principle words in tables and figures—such as nouns, pronouns, verbs, and adjectives—are capitalized. Do not capitalize connecting words and prepositions.

# 2

# WHY DOCUMENT?

When using the words or ideas of someone else, you must give credit to your source. If you fail to identify the source of the words or ideas of someone else, you are plagiarizing. Plagiarism is a form of theft—the plagiarist steals the words or ideas of someone else and claims them for his or her own. To avoid such theft, you have three options: direct quotation, paraphrase, or summary.

## Paraphrase

A paraphrase involves restating someone else's ideas in your own words, your own style, and your own sentence structure in approximately the same length as the material you are paraphrasing.

## Summary

A summary involves condensing someone else's ideas in your own words, style, and sentence structure.

# 3

# SECTIONS OF THE APA MANUSCRIPT

A manuscript written in APA style should include the following sections in the following order: title page, abstract, introduction, method, results, discussion, references, appendix, and author notes. The following is a brief description of each section.

## Title Page

The title page contains these elements in the following order:

1. Header and page number appear on every page. The page number appears in the upper right corner of the page.
2. Running head: An abbreviation of the title, of not more than 50 characters, typed in ALL CAPS. The running head is left justified and 1 inch from the top of the page (see section on running heads and headers) and appears only on the title page.

The following components of the title page are centered on the page:

3. Title of manuscript, 10 to 12 words, typed in sentence case and centered. Double-space the title if it is two or more lines in length. The title should be aesthetically pleasing in that multiple title lines should be approximately equal in length.
4. Author(s) listed without professional titles, such as *Dr*. However, whatever degrees the author holds, such as Ph.D., should

be listed. The affiliation(s) of the author(s) should also be included. Again, this information is centered.

## Abstract

The abstract should start on page 2 of the manuscript, with *Abstract* in sentence case (no italics, bold, or underlining) centered at the top. The actual abstract begins below the *Abstract* heading. The abstract of the manuscript should be a concise overview of the manuscript, containing the hypothesis/hypotheses and summaries of the method, results, and discussion sections of the manuscript. The abstract is typed in block form, meaning it is not indented, and should be equal to or less than 960 characters (roughly 120 words). All numbers included in the abstract should be in Arabic numerals; written numbers are used only to begin a sentence.

## Introduction

The introduction section of the manuscript informs the reader of several items and usually begins with an explanation of the general focus of the research or review being done and ends with a more specific, narrow explanation. Early on, the introduction includes a review of literature pertinent to the focus of the current manuscript. The literature review should be concise and assist in fully developing a background for the focus of the current manuscript. Once this background has been established, the introduction should narrow in its focus and begin relating more to the purpose/focus of the current manuscript. Hypotheses should be clearly stated, and variables should be defined. Overall, the introduction section of the manuscript should set the stage for the reader.

The introduction does not receive a label. Instead, the title of the manuscript should be typed and centered at the top of the page, with the actual text beginning after it. The introduction section should start a new page. The method, results, and discussion sections do not start new pages and should immediately follow from the previous section.

# Method

The method section of the manuscript is a detailed account of the actual research being done and should enable anyone to replicate the research without difficulty. The method section is prefaced with the word *Method* (no bold, italics, or underlining), which is centered. The method section may contain any or all of the following subheadings in sentence case, italicized, and left justified: *Participants, Materials* (or *Apparatus*), and *Procedure*.

## Participants

The participants subsection should include the sample size and pertinent demographic information (e.g., race, sex, age, etc.). Be sure to describe how the participants were recruited or selected for the research, including agreements and payments made. If using nonhuman subjects, include the genus and species or any other specific identification information. Always include a statement reporting that treatment of the participants (whether human or nonhuman) was in accordance with the ethical standards set forth by the APA.

## Materials (or Apparatus)

The materials or apparatus subsection includes a brief but detailed description and explanation of the materials (or apparatuses, if any) used in the actual research.

## Procedure

The purpose of the procedure section is to enable the reader to replicate the study, so the procedure subsection should be a brief but concise step-by-step account of how the research was carried out. All instructions should be summarized in a reasonable fashion. Begin by describing how participants were selected, randomization, how variables were manipulated, and so forth.

# Results

The results section is the component of the manuscript that provides a summary of the statistical information, information on the research design, and the outcome of the data. The results section is prefaced with the word *Results* (no bold, italics, or underlining), which is centered. The following is what you need to do to complete the results section.

- Summarize the main finding and results of the statistical data
- In specific research designs (i.e., experimental studies, descriptive studies), be sure that the summary of the data supports the conclusions stated in the paper
- Include all relevant results, but do not include individual scores from the dependant variable(s) unless, for example, they are associated with a case study
- Indicate the significance or lack of significance regarding the hypothesis
- Use tables and figures to add clarity to results
- Refer to tables and figures in the text of the paper
- Be very specific in the explanations associated with tables and figures
- In the statistical presentation report, include

  1. Inferential statistics

  2. Value of the inferential test

  3. Degrees of freedom and probability

  4. Direction of the effect

  5. Descriptive data, including measures of variability

  6. Justification of design and use of statistical test

  7. All supportive information for parametric tests, randomized-block layouts, correlational analyses, and/or nonparametric analyses

  8. Pertinent statistical power

    9. Statistical significance

    10. Effect size

## Discussion

The discussion section is prefaced with the word *Discussion* (no bold, italics, or underlining), which is centered. The discussion section of the manuscript begins with a narrow focus and ends more broadly. That is to say that the discussion should begin by stating the findings of the research and whether the hypotheses are supported. Implications of the findings should be discussed in relation to the hypotheses as well as to previous studies done (those mentioned in the introduction section). Problems, or potential problems, with the research should also be discussed. The discussion section should end with a more general presentation and the direction of future research.

## References

The reference section of the manuscript begins on a new page. The word *References* (no bold, italics, or underlining) should be centered at the top of the page. Entries in the reference list are alphabetized and should be typed as a hanging indent (the first line of the reference not indented and each succeeding line indented 1/2 inch or approximately five spaces).

## Author Notes

The author notes of the manuscript should start a new page and be labeled *Author Notes*, centered at the top of the page. These notes have several functions. Most importantly, the author notes identify the author's affiliation. Author notes also reveal sources of financial support and acknowledgment of professional contributions of colleagues. They also provide contact information for those who have further interest in the research.

# Appendix

Any appendixes to the manuscript follow the reference section. The word *Appendix* (no bold, italics, or underlining) should be centered at the top of the page and is not followed by letters or numbers. Use letters only to discriminate between multiple appendixes, if any are present. Outline the materials presented in the appendix left-flushed under the appendix label. The appendix may include figure captions, figures, tables, printed materials used, computer printouts of data, and so forth. This first page is merely a list of what the appendix section contains.

# 4

# Miscellaneous Rules of APA Format

## Running Head

The running head of a manuscript is a summary of the title of the manuscript. The running head should not exceed 50 characters, including spaces between words. On the title page, the running head appears as *Running head:* and is followed by the actual abbreviated title in ALL CAPS. The running head is located 1 inch from the top of the page (standard margin).

**Example:**
Running head: ABBREVIATED TITLE OF ARTICLE

## Header

The purpose of the header is to identify and organize the actual pages of the unpublished manuscript when the publisher's editors are reviewing it. The header should be the first 2 to 3 words of the title. The header is located 1/2 inch from the top of the page, followed five spaces later by the page number. It is right justified. The easiest way to situate the page number within the header in most word-processing programs is to type the header left justified, space over five times, insert the page number, and finally right-justify the entire header.

**Example:**
Brief Header of Article 1

# Headings for Tables

Column headings in tables identify the information presented in the table. These headings enable the reader to follow the data in an organized manner. Headings should be brief and identify the data that follows. APA format uses several levels of column headings:

- Level I: Column heads, cover one column
- Level II: Column spanners, cover two or more columns
- Level III: Decked heads, stacking of heading

**Example: Level I**

```
Marriage
```

**Example: Level II**

```
Marriages  Marriages

  First       Second
```

**Example: Level III**

```
        Marriage

First          Second
```

# Figures: Graphs and Tables

When deciding whether to use a figure (i.e., charts, drawings, graphs, tables, etc.), always remember that figures should be used only to illustrate main points made within the manuscript. In this section of the manuscript, tables are columns and rows of numbers that report data, and figures primarily refer to graphs.

Here are the basic formatting rules used with figures:

- Figures must not "overshoot" the standard 1-inch margin
- Figure titles should be brief and to the point
- All figures must be referred to within the text of the manuscript
- Be consistent!

When deciding to use a *table,* keep the following in mind:

- Tables are double-spaced, with a 12-point font
- The length of the table should be 3/4 the width (e.g., if the width of the table is 4 inches, the length should be 3 inches)
- Each row and column should be labeled
- Headings used for columns are centered at the top of the column
- If the purpose of the first column of a table is to define variables, then that column is left justified; the following columns (those reporting statistics) are right justified
- Do not bold or italicize labels or numbers within the table

# 5

# Abbreviations for APA Format

The primary reason for using abbreviations is to clarify and simplify writing. When deciding to abbreviate, consider the following:

1. Will the abbreviation reduce repetition?
2. Is there a standard abbreviation for the term?
3. Does the abbreviation lend itself to clarity and simplicity?

When choosing to abbreviate terms, remember that overusing abbreviations can confuse the reader and hinder comprehension. In addition, abbreviations used fewer than three times should be omitted from the manuscript, because they may be hard for the reader to remember. The purpose of abbreviations is to clarify and simplify.

## The How's of Abbreviation

The term that is to be abbreviated must first be identified (spelled out) in the text and then be followed by the abbreviation in parentheses. Once the term has been identified, it is then appropriate to use the abbreviation throughout the remainder of the manuscript without any further spelling-out of the term.

> NOTE: Abbreviations cannot start a sentence. Always spell out the term when beginning a sentence.

## Figures and Tables

Abbreviations used in figures must be identified in the legend or caption. Abbreviations used in tables must be identified in the title of the table or in a table note.

Some minor rules apply to the use and placement of the period ( . ) with abbreviations. Use a period with initials representing names, when abbreviating *the United States,* with Latin abbreviations, and with reference abbreviations. However, do not use periods with state abbreviations, capital letter abbreviations, or with measurement abbreviations.

> NOTE: When abbreviating the word *inch,* it is appropriate to use a period to avoid confusing the abbreviation with the preposition *in.*

## Forming the Plural

To form the plural of an abbreviation, add *s* without an apostrophe.

> NOTE: Units of measurements are generally not pluralized. To make the abbreviation for *page* plural, however, use *pp.,* not *pgs.*

## Useful Latin Abbreviations

| | | | |
|---|---|---|---|
| cf. | compare | i.e. | that is |
| e.g. | for example | viz. | namely |
| etc. | and so forth | vs. | versus, against |

# 6

# QUOTATIONS

All material taken directly from any other document must be enclosed in quotation marks. Keep in mind the following:

- Use double quotation marks when quoting material found in text; use single quotation marks if a quote is included in the original quoted material (see Example 1).
- When referring to a document in the text of the manuscript, provide the author's name, date of publication, and page number(s) all in parentheses.
- Include the reference source on the reference page. All quoted material should be accurate.
- Cite references immediately following the quotation.
- It is the author's responsibility to decide if permission is needed to quote another person. Permission is not needed to quote from APA-copyrighted journals, as long as the quotation does not exceed 500 words.

**Example 1**

The last experiment that included

freshmen in a psychology class failed to

support the hypotheses. Marvin Thompson

responded to questions concerning this

```
study by saying, "often this is expected

when a convenient sample is used"

(Thompson, 1979, p. 13).
```

- Include quotations up to 40 words in the text of the manuscript.
- When the passage being quoted is longer than 40 words, create a block style paragraph by executing the following steps:
  1. Start the quotation on a new line
  2. Indent five spaces (1/2 inch) from the left margin
  3. Do not use quotation marks; type material within this blocked format
  4. For paragraphs included in the block, indent the paragraph five spaces from the margin of the quoted material
  5. All materials are double-spaced

**Example 2**

```
Teall (1971) wrote,

    One of the most important men in the early

    exploration of Oklahoma never saw Oklahoma

    himself. The man was Estevanico—sometimes

    called Estevan or Stephen. Estevanico was a

    black man, and while much is known about

    the last years of his life and his death,

    little is known about his birth or his

    early years. (p. 7)
```

- When omitting anything from quoted material, use three ellipses points.

**Example 3:**

Carol's new car has a number of options: seat warmers, special headlights, . . . all included in the 2001 model.

# 7

# REFERENCING IN APA FORMAT

Basic rules of referencing:

- Do not indent the first line of a reference entry, because each entry needs to have a hanging indent. Indent the succeeding line(s) 1/2 inch (five spaces).
- Double-space all references.
- Alphabetize references according to the first author's last name. Use the second author's last name to continue alphabetizing only if the first author's name is listed in the reference section more than once. If no author is listed, alphabetize according to the title of whatever is being referenced.
- Use periods after the author's first and middle initials.
- Space one time after each period in the references to conserve space.

## Periodical

```
Last Name, Initial(s) (Year/Date of

    Publication). Title of article is listed

    here. Name of Journal, volume number(issue

    number), page numbers.
```

*Last Name, Initial(s):* List all authors of the publication in the order they are listed on the actual publication. Spell out the last name(s) and follow with the first initial (and middle initial if given). In the case of multiple authors, list all authors using the ampersand symbol ( & ) to separate the next to last and last author's names.

This format for authorship applies to all referencing. The exception to this format is authorship without specific individuals, such as no author.

*Year/Date of Publication:* Type the year in parentheses. Occasionally, a month or season, depending on the publication, will be given. In the latter case, type the year first followed by a comma and then the month or season.

*Title:* Type the full title of the article. Capitalize only the first word of the title and any proper nouns. If there is a subtitle, conclude the title with a colon ( : ), and capitalize the first letter of the first word of the subtitle.

*Name of Journal: Italicize* the full name of the journal in which the article appeared. Follow the name of the journal with a comma.

*Volume Number and Issue Number: Italicize* the journal's volume number. If the journal citation does not list an issue number, follow the volume number with a comma. When an issue number is listed, the volume number should be followed immediately with the issue number in parentheses, *not italicized*, followed by a comma.

*Page Numbers:* Type the page number(s) separated by an en dash ( – ), concluding with a period.

Burris, K., & Berry, Z. (1980). The life and

times of Mary. *Evolution, 61*(9), 491–499.

## Entire/Special Section of a Journal

Brown, A. E. (Ed.). (1996). The rules of play

in Special Olympics [Special issue]. *The*

*Journal of Sport Psychology, 300*(5).

If the issue has no editor(s), the title moves to the first position in the citation.

## *Magazine Article*

References to articles in magazines are similar to periodicals with only one difference. When typing the year/date of publication, include the year, month, and day (if given).

## *Monograph with Issue Numbers and Serial (or Whole) Number*

Gray, B. T., & Watson, K. (2005). Time

    management with couples with dual careers.

    *Monograph in the Studies on Careers in the*

    *New Millennium, 23*(Serial No. 50).

*The word* whole *can be used interchangeably with* serial.

## *Monograph Bound into a Journal with Continuous Pagination*

Kappa, A. C., & Booker, R. B., Jr. (2000). The

    life and times of women denied education

    in third world countries [Monograph]. *The*

    *International Journal on Women's Studies,*

    *133,* 201-220.

*Use brackets to identify the literary form.*

## Newsletter Article

References to an article from a newsletter follow the same format as those to a general periodical.

Schmidt, I. M. (1987, Fall). Parenting styles

applied to today's generation. *Parenting*

*Psychology, 13,* 3-6.

## Daily/Weekly Newspaper Article

References to newspaper articles are similar to magazines with only one difference. Page numbers are preceded by *p.* or *pp.* If page numbers are discontinuous, list all page numbers, separating the page numbers with commas.

Brixey, J. (2000, May 5). Environmental

factors in biology shed light on insurance

claims. *The Houston Weekly,* p. C4.

## Abstract from a Secondary Source (Print Periodical):

Hornet, O. L., Winn, Q., & Mills, Z. (1999).

Racial bias: In seniors with English as a

second language. *Seniors Today, 12,* 81-85.

Abstract obtained form *PsycNet:*

*Developmental Psychology,* 2000, *4,* Abstract

No. 501.

Secondary sources are often found within a primary source of reference—books, articles, papers, and so forth.

## Book

```
Last Name, Initial(s). (Year of Publication).

    Title of book goes here (edition).

    Location of Publisher: Name of Publisher.
```

*Year of Publication:* List the year that the book was published.

*Edition:* If the book includes an edition, which is usually a number, enclose it in parentheses immediately following the title of the book. Use the abbreviation of *ed.* when listing the edition's number. Do not italicize the information regarding the edition.

*Location of Publisher:* Type the city and state (or country if outside the United States), followed by a colon ( : ). The exception to listing city and state is when the city is well known (e.g., San Francisco, New York, London).

*Name of Publisher:* Identify the publishing company that published the book, followed by a period.

```
Mitchell, J. (1982). The mythos of

    homosexuality (2nd ed.). London: Express

    Publishers.
```

### *Article or Chapter in an Edited Book*

```
Last Name, Initial(s). (Year of Publication).

    Title of article or book chapter goes

    here. In Initial(s)., Last Name (Eds.),
```

*Title of book* (page numbers). Location of

Publisher: Name of Publisher.

*In Initials., Last Name:* The name(s) of the book's editor(s) are listed reversed, the first and middle initials precede the last name.

*Page numbers:* Preface the page numbers with *pp.*, or *p.* if information is found on one page.

Bond, V. (1980). The psychology of life:

Working with blended families. In J. Wynn,

Jr., M. White, & M. Boat (Eds.), *Family*

*psychology* (pp. 27-36). Boston: Brooks.

*In case no author or editor is listed, alphabetize (excluding* a, an, *and* the*) the entry according to the title of the book, still italicized, in the place where the author's name would be listed.*

*When referencing the* Diagnostic and Statistical Manual of Mental Disorders, *use the following basic citation reference, filling in the necessary information:*

American Psychiatric Association. (19xx).

*Diagnostic and statistical manual of mental*

*disorders* (xx ed.). Washington, DC: Author.

*Publication Information:* DSM–III     (1980)  3rd ed.

DSM–III – R  (1987)  3rd ed., revised

DSM–IV     (1994)  4th ed.

DSM–IV–TR  (2000)  text revision

## *Encyclopedia or Dictionary*

Arnold, P., & Loftis, E. (1994). Curriculum.

In *The world book encyclopedia* (Vol. 4,

pp. 301-311). New York: World Book

Encyclopedia.

Chandler, J. (1990). *The Dictionary of*

*pediatric medicine* (9th ed., Vol. 5). San

Francisco: Smith.

## Brochure

Last Name, Initial(s). (Year of Publication).

*Title of brochure* [Brochure]. Location of

Publisher: Name of Publisher.

*Reference a brochure as if it were a book. Note that* Brochure *is typed in brackets following the edition.*

Christie, A., Capp, W., & Goyle, C. J. (1976).

*A basic approach to cardiovascular disease*

(2nd ed.) [Brochure]. St. Louis: Mandalay.

# Technical or Research Report

Crawford, G. P., & Parks, L. C. (2001).

    *Variability in delinquent behavior among*

    *incarcerated juveniles* (Diagnostic and

    Evaluation Rep. No. 236). Dallas, TX: Conn

    Publishing.

*References to technical or research reports follow the same format as those for general periodicals with only one difference. The report number (if available) is included in parentheses directly after the title.*

# Report as an Article or Chapter in an Edited Edition

Tolouse, J. Z., Union, B., & Tion, C. A.

    (2003, August). Identification of

    subconscious thought pattern in infants

    with fetal alcohol disorder. In K. R.

    Whitter & W. M. Starr (Eds.), *Cognitive*

    *factors related to infant development* (NIH

    Publication No. 32-9311, pp. 24-45). New

    York: U.S. Department of Child Welfare.

# Proceedings Published Regularly

Nichols, M., & Boyd, G. H. (2006). Using

Functional Magnetic Resonance Imaging

(fMRI) to identify soft tissue mass.

*Proceedings of the Regional Radiological*

*Society, 33,* 876-890.

*The same format is used for meetings, symposiums, and periodicals.*

# Unpublished Contribution to a Symposium

Constantine, P. A. (1998, April). Use of

assessment measures with children with

PTSD. In J. B. Voyce (Chair), *Cognitive*

*behavioral assessment of children with*

*anxiety disorders.* Symposium conducted at

the meeting of the American Pediatric

Organization, Los Angeles.

*Include the group providing the symposium.*

# Dissertation or Theses Abstract

*Dissertations and Master's theses are referenced in the same format.*

## Published Doctoral or Master's Dissertation

Last Name, Initial(s). (Year of Publication).

Title of dissertation. *Dissertation/Masters*

*Abstracts International, volume number*

(issue number if given), page number.

*If the dissertation is retrieved from microfilm, follow the page number with the following information contained in parentheses:* University Microfilms No. XXXXX-XXXXX. *End the citation with a period.*

Eden, D. K. (1971). Cost accounting: The

necessary core in accounting. *Dissertations*

*Abstracts International, 35*(X51007), 1981E.

## Unpublished Doctoral or Master's Dissertation

Last Name, Initial(s). (Year Written). *Title of*

*dissertation.* Unpublished doctoral/master's

dissertation, Name of University, City of

University, State.

*Title of Dissertation:* Note that the title, including the concluding period, should be *italicized.*

Cunby, D. (1985). *Dentistry and the stress*

*placed on children.* Unpublished doctoral

dissertation, University of California,

Davis.

## Review of Book/Film/Video

Last Name, Initial(s). (Year of Publication).

Title of review [Review of the

book/film/video *Title of Book/Film/Video*].

*Name of Journal, volume number*(issue

number), page numbers.

*Title of Review:* If a title is not given for the actual review, use the information inside the brackets as the title.

Ravencroft, A. (2001). NRMs in children's

cartoons [Review of the film *The Witch of*

*Riverbend*]. *Journal of Children's Media, 1,*

4-6.

## Unpublished Paper Presented at a Meeting

Last Name, Initial(s). (Year of Meeting,

Month). *Title of unpublished paper.* Paper

presented at the meeting of Title of

Meeting, City, State.

*Title of Meeting:* Insert the title of the meeting.

Bowmen, E. (2001, May). *Stress and daily*

   *hassles.* Paper presented at the meeting of

   the Association for International Medi-

   cine, Chicago, IL.

## Poster Session

Last Name, Initial(s). (Year of session,

   Month). *Title of poster.* Poster session

   presented at the annual meeting of the

   Name of Organization Sponsoring Session,

   City, State.

*Name of Organization Sponsoring Session:* Insert the name of the
organization that sponsored the poster session.

Carlos, N. A. (1999, September). *Diversity in*

   *the U.S.* Poster session presented at the

   regional meeting of the Multicultural

   Society of America, Denver, CO.

## Unpublished Manuscript Not Submitted for Publication

Last Name, Initial(s). (Year manuscript was

    written). *Title of unpublished manuscript.*

    Unpublished manuscript.

Griggs, Z., & Johnson, V. (1994). *Seniors*

    *adults: Pedagogical strategies for teaching*

    *computer technology.* Unpublished manuscript.

## Electronic Media
### *On-line Journal*

Last Name, Initial(s). (Year of Publication).

    Title of article. *Name of Periodical.*

    Retrieved Month day, year, from

    http://specify path here

*Specify path here:* Insert the Web address from which the article came. If the article is retrieved via file transfer protocol (ftp), replace *http* with *ftp*.

Smart, K. (1991). Computer data on-line.

 *Computers Today*. Retrieved August 29,

 1999, from http://www.comptoday.com

## On-line Newsletter

References to on-line newsletters follow the same format as those to on-line articles.

McDermott, P. S. (1999, October). The use of

 meditation for simple phobias. *Empirical*

 *News*. Retrieved April 19, 2001, from

 http://www.empiricalnews.net

## Newsgroup, On-line Forum and Discussion Group, and Electronic Mailing List

Artisson, R. G. (1999, October 31). Pagan

 culture in western society [Msg 1324].

 Message posted to

 http://www.groups.diversity.org

*Include the specific message number.*

## Message Posted to an Electronic Mailing List

Sourgh, T., & Adams, N. R. (1998, May 2). Why

 are we here in limbo? [Msg 77]. Message

 posted to Existential Therapists

electronic mailing list, archived at

http://w3.chileanclinicians.com/archives/

existential/msg77.htm

## Abstract on CD-ROM

Last Name, Initial(s). (Year of Publication).

Title of article. [CD-ROM]. *Title of*

*Journal, Volume Number*(issue number).

Abstract from: Source and Retrieval Number.

Thomas, D. C., & Chalon, A. E. (1954). Will

computers become a tool in the future?

[CD-ROM]. *Business Chronicle, 63*. Abstract

from: Business File: Abstract Item: R19510.

- *Always provide enough information in on-line referencing so that repeated retrieval is possible.*
- *Specify the specific source of the material (i.e., Web site, e-mail, abstract, CD-ROM, or database).*

## Television Broadcast

Last Name, Initial(s). (Position of author).

(Year, Month day of broadcast). *Title of*

*television program* [Television broadcast].

```
City, State of Distributor: Name of

    Broadcasting Company.
```

*Position of author:* Place the official title of the author, writer, producer, etc. in parentheses (i.e., producer, director, etc.) after the name.

```
Brooks. T. (Executive Producer). (1999,

    November 2). 60 Minutes [Television

    broadcast]. New York: Columbia Broadcasting.
```

## Television Series

```
Last Name, Initial(s). (Producer). (Year of

    Broadcast). Title of television series

    [Television series]. City, State of

    Distributor: Name of Broadcasting Company.
```

*Alphabetize the entry by the last name of the producer.*

```
Shelton, W. (Producer). (1997). City in focus

    [Television series]. Los Angeles: American

    Broadcasting Company.
```

## Single Episode from a Television Series

```
Whipple, D. R. (Writer), & Mudscone, T. B.

    (Director). (2000). He's going down
```

[Television series episode]. In J. J.

Walker (Producer), *Living on the inside.*

Polka, Nebraska: Quads Broadcasting.

## Music Recording

Livingston, J. C. (2000). Life is but a dream

[Recorded by J. T. Cuervo]. On *My highway*

[Cassette]. Nashville, TN. (2002)

*The name(s) of the recording artist(s) are listed reversed, the first and middle initials precede the last name. Identify the medium type on which the recording was done, such as CD, cassette, etc.*

## Audio Recording

Stifler, M. M. (Speaker). (2005). *Writing*

*formats for pediatric developmental*

*counselors* (CD Recording No. 13-998A).

Norfolk, VA: Developmental Pediatric

Society.

# 8

# EXAMPLE APA MANUSCRIPT

The following paper, "Attitudes Towards Disabled Individuals as Influenced by Gender and Disability Type," by Jimmy L. Widdifield, Jr., is a research paper in APA style.

Effects of Gender and Disability Type    1

Running head: EFFECTS OF GENDER AND DISABILITY TYPE

Attitudes Toward Disabled Individuals as Influenced by Gender and Disability Type

Jimmy L. Widdifield, Jr.
University of Central Oklahoma

Effects of Gender and Disability Type    2

Abstract

The purpose of this study is to determine the attitude displayed toward permanently and temporarily physically disabled individuals and whether gender was an influencing factor. Participants viewed a variety of video vignettes depicting different levels of disability and then rated the confederate in the vignette on competency, knowledge, and how comfortable interaction would be with the confederate. These characteristics were combined to make a composite score. Analysis of the composite score indicated no negative attitude was present toward the confederate, regardless of disability and participant gender. However, when the characteristics were individually analyzed, a significant interaction was found for knowledge and a main effect for gender in the comfortability condition.

Attitudes Toward Disabled
Individuals as Influenced by
Gender and Disability Type

A multitude of research has centered on
discrimination based on age, race, and sex. More
recently, though, research on discriminatory
attitudes has focused on the disabled, and more
importantly, the physically disabled. This
research has found that a negative attitude is
held by able-bodied individuals toward the
physically disabled population (Ficten & Amsel,
1986). Also, Ryan (1981) found that the physically
disabled are presumed to be inferior on some
dimensions and not others due to the disability
and depending on the situation and context. As
more physically disabled individuals are
encountered in work and academic settings, it is
important that society understands what kind of
individuals they are and are not. Disabled people
are like anyone else, with the exception of their
specific disability. They are not helpless but are
able to lead relatively normal lives—they marry,

Effects of Gender and Disability Type     4

have children, own homes and automobiles, and
pursue professional and academic careers.

Physical disability can be defined as an
imputed physical defect or imperfection that is
assumed to limit the capacity of an individual to
engage in "normal" physical activity (Ryan, 1981).
Physical disabilities are present in one of two
forms, permanent or temporary. For the purpose of
this study, permanent physical disability is one
in which individuals are immobile due to paralysis
and are thus confined to a wheelchair. Temporary
physical disability is a condition in which
individuals have incurred an injury and must
utilize a wheelchair until healing has taken
place. The point of this study is to determine
whether negative attitudes are present toward
these two forms of physical disability and whether
gender has an influence on these attitudes. Also,
this study is a replication of a previous study
done by Ford and Callicoat in 1991, which focused
on negative attitudes toward individuals with a
permanent disability. It is important to note that
evaluations of the physically disabled can be more

Effects of Gender and Disability Type     5

extreme than those of able-bodied individuals
(Bailey, 1991).

Ford & Callicoat (1991) conducted research on
attitudes toward disabled individuals. The
researchers presented a confederate in one of
three experimental conditions utilizing a
wheelchair. These conditions depicted the
confederate to be permanently, temporarily, or not
disabled. Participants were asked to rate the
confederate on competence, helpfulness, and how
comfortable interaction with the confederate was.
What the researchers found was that a negative
attitude did exist when the wheelchair was
present. Also discovered was that females gave
fewer positive responses than males.

Negative attitudes toward physically disabled
individuals have also been found in several other
studies. Stovall & Sedlacek (1983) found the
expression of negative attitudes toward physically
disabled individuals. Here, participants formed
negative attitudes to physically disabled
individuals depending on the level of disability
(permanent or temporary) and the situation in

which the disabled person was encountered. Situations in which close contact with a disabled person was required revealed the existence of negative attitudes. Close contact here could be defined as a personal relationship. However, researchers also found that a positive attitude existed toward physically disabled individuals in academic settings and that females reacted more positively toward physically disabled individuals. Royal & Roberts (1987) also found that females expressed a more positive and accepting attitude toward individuals with a physical disability than did males. These findings suggest that attitudes toward disabled individuals are influenced by gender.

Contact with physically disabled individuals is also avoided (Ficten & Amsel, 1986). People seem to seek out companionship and contact with other individuals they perceive as similar to themselves. This has implications that can be applied to how comfortable an individual would be interacting with a person with a disability. Ficten & Amsel (1986) also found that less socially desirable traits were attributed to physically disabled individuals. These traits were, not surprisingly, the opposite of those traits attributed to able-bodied individuals.

Another area of research that can be generalized is employment potential. Ravaud, Madiot, & Ville (1992) found that qualified able-bodied applicants were more likely than physically disabled counterparts to receive a more favorable response by potential employers. Christman & Slaten (1991), however, found that physically disabled applicants were rated more favorably than able-bodied counterparts on employment characteristics and management potential scales. No explanation has been offered as to why this discrepancy exists.

Despite the large body of research conducted on the physically disabled, one population has been overlooked—the temporarily disabled. Negative attitudes toward the permanently disabled have been firmly established, but does this attitude generalize to these individuals? It is hypothesized that temporarily physically disabled individuals will be rated higher on a combination of characteristics than physically disabled individuals. Also being hypothesized is that gender of the participant will influence the ratings ascribed.

## Method

### Participants

Participants in this study consisted of 218 university students (females = 127, males = 91). Participants were recruited through the General Psychology Subject Pool on campus, and the mean age equaled 19.8 years. Participants received one credit for their participation, therefore aiding them to fulfill a course requirement. Treatment of participants was in accordance with the ethical standards of the American Psychological Association.

### Materials

Three video vignettes were taped on a VHS tape. According to Weisel & Florian (1990), females with disabilities were regarded with a less positive attitude than males with

Effects of Gender and Disability Type    9

disabilities. Therefore, a 22-year-old male
confederate was used to read a script about basic
cardiopulmonary resuscitation (CPR) techniques.
The vignettes depicted the confederate in one of
three conditions: (1) seated in a wheelchair,
implying a permanent disability; (2) seated in a
wheelchair with one leg extended out and wearing
an ankle brace, implying a temporary disability;
or (3) standing, implying no disability.

Two questionnaires were also utilized. The
first was an eight-question quiz over the material
presented in the video. The second was a
five-question instrument concerning different
components of the video and utilized Likert scales
for each question. Of importance in this
instrument were three questions concerning the
participants' feelings about the confederate in
the video. These questions focused on the
perceived competency and knowledge of the
confederate as well as how comfortable
the participant would be interacting with the
confederate. Participants were also asked to
indicate their age and sex on the survey.

*Procedure*

Experimental sessions were conducted during a two week period in order to obtain a sufficient number of participants. Sessions were given in 30-minute intervals, each lasting a maximum of 15 minutes. The remaining 15 minutes were used to score the participants' answers to the two questionnaires presented, as well as to re-cue the videotape. Once the participants were present and seated, credit slips were issued, and a brief explanation was given about the experimental session. Participants were told they would be viewing a brief video concerning basic CPR techniques followed by a quiz and survey. Participants were also asked to remain after they finished so that a more detailed explanation of the research could be given.

Participants then viewed one of the three video vignettes. Determination of which vignette shown was chosen randomly. After the video vignette ended, the questionnaires were administered. Once all participants finished, the

researcher collected the questionnaires and credit
slips. The participants were then told the current
research focused on attitudes toward people with
disabilities. Also, participants were invited to
leave their name and address if they were
interested in obtaining results of the research.
Participants were then dismissed.

## Results

Table 1 displays composite scores that were
obtained by adding the individual scores of
competency, knowledge, and how comfortable
interaction would be. Data were then analyzed
using a 2 (Gender)$\times$33 (Level of Disability)
between subjects ANOVA. Table 1 shows that no
significance for main effects was found as well as
no interaction. Each component of the composite
score was then analyzed. No significance was found
in the competency component. However, a
significant interaction $F$, (2, 212) = 5.525,
$p<0.0046$ was found between gender and level of
disability (see Figure 2). Simple effects analysis

was performed to determine where the difference would be found. Table 2a shows that significance was found at Gender at Permanent $F$, $(1, 212)$ = 5.460, p<3.890 and Disability at Male $F$, $(2, 212)$ = 3.760, p<3.040. Gender at Permanent showed a lower mean for females (M = 7.456) than for males (M = 9.936). Means for Disability at Male showed the permanent condition highest (M = 9.936), followed by N/A (M = 7.350) and temporary (M = 7.333). Significance was also found for the comfortability component for the Gender factor ($F$, $(1, 212)$ = 4.100, p<0.0441). Means here reveal females = 9.696 and males = 8.545 (see Table 3).

## Discussion

The hypotheses of current research were (1) a more negative attitude would be present in the permanent physical disability condition and no negative attitude would exist in the temporary disability condition or N/A condition and (2) gender would influence attitudes attributed to the permanent physical disability condition. Findings for the overall composite score showed that a negative attitude was not present toward the

permanent condition or the other two levels of

disability. Also, gender had no influence on

attitudes displayed toward the confederate in the

permanent physical disability condition for the

composite score. When the composite score was

broken into its components of competency,

knowledge, and how likely comfortable interaction

would be, some interesting results were found. An

interaction between gender and level of disability

was present within the knowledge component.

Analyses found that males perceived the

permanently disabled confederate to be more

knowledgeable than did females and that males

perceived the permanently disabled confederate to

more knowledgeable than the temporarily or non-

disabled confederate. Females rated themselves to

be more likely to interact with the confederate

without regard to level of disability.

    Results of this study seem to follow the

inconsistency of previous research. Ford and

Callicoat's (1991) findings suggested that a

Effects of Gender and Disability Type    14

negative attitude did exist toward the permanently

disabled concerning knowledge, helpfulness, and

how comfortable interaction would be between

participants and someone who is permanently and

physically disabled. In addition to this finding,

they also found females gave less positive

responses than did males. In contrast, no negative

attitude was found toward the permanently disabled

in the current study. Another inconsistency with

Ford and Callicoat's findings is current research

found that males were more likely than females to

perceive the permanently disabled as more

knowledgeable. Even within the male group, the

permanently disabled were perceived as more

knowledgeable than those at the other two levels

of disability, temporary and non-disabled.

Findings of this study are also inconsistent

with research done by Stovall and Sedlacek (1983),

Royal and Roberts (1983), and Ficten and Amsel

(1986). These studies all found some degree of

negative attitude expressed toward the physically

disabled. Stovall and Sedlacek's findings and

current findings are inconsistent for the effects

of gender; previous research found females to be
more positive than males toward the permanently
physically disabled. The current study found
somewhat of the opposite, with males responding
more favorably than females. This same
inconsistency is also found when looking at Royal
and Roberts's previous research (1987). Ficten and
Amsel (1983) reported findings that contact with
the physically disabled is often avoided. Current
findings are interesting concerning this issue.
Females were found to be more comfortable
interacting with the confederate no matter the
level of disability, suggesting that contact with
the permanently disabled confederate is not
avoided significantly.

Findings of this study can also be compared to
research done on disability and employment.
Because the permanently disabled are seen as more
knowledgeable, as indicated by this study, results
are consistent with research done by Ravaud,
Madiot, and Ville (1992) as well as research done
by Christman and Slaten (1991).

With previous research being inconsistent and findings of this study not agreeing or disagreeing with that previous research, it is difficult to state that a negative attitude toward the physically disabled (permanent or temporary) exists. Why do these inconsistencies exist? Possible explanations could be the level of interaction with the disabled and/or personal experience of being disabled. Ficten and Amsel (1986) found that contact with the disabled is avoided. This alone could perpetuate a negative attitude because absence of interaction does not allow people to get to know the disabled on a personal level, beyond the stereotypes.

The finding of no significance in this study could be due to methodological effects. The video vignettes showed the confederate reading from a script; this alone could affect how participants perceived the confederate. Also, participants were left to assume the confederate was either permanently or temporarily physically disabled. Allowing for this assumption could have led the participants to reach the wrong conclusion, thus interfering with the rating of the confederate.

Findings of this study could be viewed in several ways. Finding that no negative attitude exists toward the disabled could imply that mainstreaming efforts to curb discrimination are showing success. Of interest was that males responded more favorably than females toward the disabled. Historically, females have responded more favorably to disadvantaged groups, thus leaving this researcher to conclude again that mainstreaming efforts have been successful with males. Further research could focus on the differences between males and females.

References

Bailey, J. W. (1991). Evaluation of a task partner

who does or does not have a physical disability:

Response amplification or sympathy effect? [CD-

ROM]. *Rehabilitation Psychology, 36*(2), 99-110.

Abstract from: WinSpurs: PsychLIT Item: 1992-

05957-001.

Christman, L. A., & Slaten, B. L. (1991). Attitudes

toward people with disabilities and judgment of

employment potential. *Perceptual and Motor

Skills, 72*(2), 467-475.

Ficten, C. S., & Amsel, R. (1986). Trait attributions

about college students with a physical

disability: Circumplex analyses and

methodological issues. *Journal of Applied

Social Psychology, 16*(5), 410-427.

Effects of Gender and Disability Type    19

Ford & Callicoat (1991, May). *Effect of perceived*

   *handicap of competency of the instructor.* Poster

   session presented at the biannual Student Poster

   Session, Edmond, OK.

Ravaud, J. F., Madiot, B., & Ville, I. (1992).

   Discrimination towards disabled people seeking

   employment. *Social Science and Medicine, 35*(8),

   951-958.

Royal, G. P., & Roberts, M. C. (1987). Students'

   perceptions of and attitudes toward

   disabilities: A comparison of twenty

   conditions. *Journal of Clinical Child*

   *Psychology, 16*(2), 122-132.

Ryan, K. M. (1981). Developmental differences in

   reactions to the physically disabled. *Human*

   *Development, 24*(4), 240-256.

Stovall, C., & Sedlacek, W. E. (1983). Attitudes of

   male and female university students with

different physical disabilities. *Journal of College Student Personnel, 27*(4), 39-47.

Weisel, A., & Florian, V. (1990). Same- and cross-gender attitudes toward persons with physical disabilities [CD-ROM]. *Rehabilitation Psychology, 35*(4). Abstract from: WinSpurs: PsychLIT Item: 1991-27992-001.

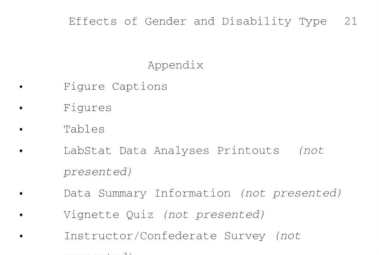

Effects of Gender and Disability Type    21

Appendix

- Figure Captions
- Figures
- Tables
- LabStat Data Analyses Printouts    *(not presented)*
- Data Summary Information *(not presented)*
- Vignette Quiz *(not presented)*
- Instructor/Confederate Survey *(not presented)*

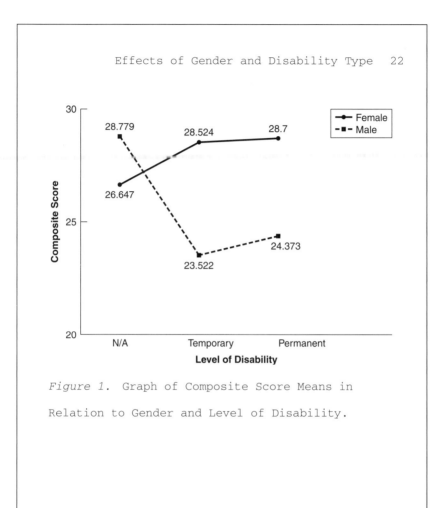

*Figure 1.* Graph of Composite Score Means in Relation to Gender and Level of Disability.

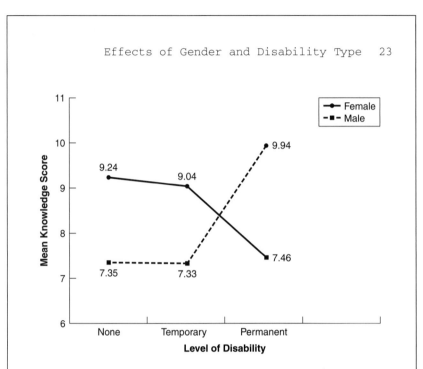

Effects of Gender and Disability Type    23

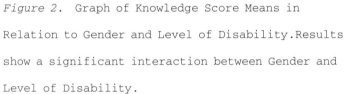

*Figure 2.* Graph of Knowledge Score Means in Relation to Gender and Level of Disability.Results show a significant interaction between Gender and Level of Disability.

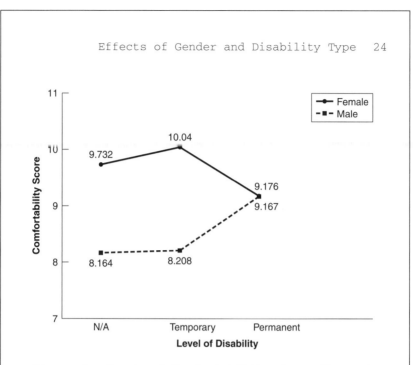

Effects of Gender and Disability Type   24

*Figure 3.* Graph of Comfortability Score Means in Relation to Gender and Level of Disability.Results show a main effect for Gender.

Table 1  *Composite Scores*

| Source | SS | df | MS | F | p |
|---|---|---|---|---|---|
| Total | 24409.021 | 217 | | | |
| GENDER | 294.228 | 1 | 294.228 | 2.657 | 0.1046 |
| LEVEL OF DISABILITY | 102.273 | 2 | 51.136 | 0.462 | 0.6308 |
| A × B | 528.549 | 2 | 264.274 | 2.387 | 0.0944 |
| Error Between | 23472.856 | 212 | 110.721 | | |

Effects of Gender and Disability Type    24

Table 2  *Knowledge Scores*

| Source | SS | df | MS | F | p |
|--------|-----|-----|-----|-----|-----|
| Total | 4220.994 | 217 | | | |
| GENDER | 7.126 | 1 | 7.126 | 0.378 | 0.5395 |
| LEVEL OF DISABILITY | 9.785 | 2 | 4.896 | 0.259 | 0.7718 |
| A × B | 208.439 | 2 | 104.219 | 5.525 | 0.0046 |
| Error Between | 399.182 | 212 | 18.864 | | |

Table 2a  *Simple Effects of Knowledge Scores*

| Source | SS | df | MS | F | p |
|--------|-----|-----|-----|-----|-----|
| GENDER | 216.09 | 3 | | | |
|   at Permanent | 103.01 | 1 | 103.01 | 5.46 | 3.89 |
|   at Temporary | 60.53 | 1 | 60.53 | 3.21 | 3.89 |
|   at N/A | 52.55 | 1 | 52.55 | 2.79 | 3.89 |
| LEVEL OF DISABILITY | 213.08 | 4 | | | |
|   at Female | 71.27 | 2 | 35.64 | 1.89 | 3.04 |
|   at Male | 141.81 | 2 | 70.91 | 3.76 | 3.04 |
| Error Between | 3999.18 | 212 | 18.86 | | |

Table 3  *Comfortability Scores*

| Source | SS | df | MS | F | p |
|--------|-----|-----|-----|-----|-----|
| Total | 3487.967 | 217 | | | |
| GENDER | 65.425 | 1 | 65.425 | 4.100 | 0.0441 |
| LEVEL OF DISABILITY | 1.854 | 2 | 0.927 | 0.058 | 0.9436 |
| A × B | 32.672 | 2 | 16.336 | 1.024 | 0.3610 |
| Error Between | 3383.179 | 212 | 15.958 | | |

# 9

# GRAMMAR

## Apostrophes

There are two reasons to use apostrophes:

- To show possession
- To contract

### *Possession*

The English language is very regular about showing possession. In fact, English has no "exceptional" possessives. In other words, we use *'s* or *'* without fail.

- Use *'s* after a **singular noun**:

    John's boat

    the player's fault

    James's garden

    the dog's bowl

    Mary's coat

    her friend's brother

- Use *'* after a **plural noun**:

    the cats' dishes (dishes belonging to more than one cat)

    the Smiths' car (a car owned by more than one Smith)

the students' assignments (the assignments of the students)

- Use *'s* after irregular plurals:

  the men's suits

  the children's toys

  the women's project

## Tricky Points

- Although the plural of **brother-in-law** is **brothers-in-law,** the possessive is **brother-in-law's.** The possessive plural is **brothers-in-law's.**

### Names that end in *-s:*

- Mr. Thomas owns a home. That home is **Mr. Thomas's** home.
- Mr. and Mrs. Williams have a home. That home is the **Williamses'** home. (The tricky point here is that the proper noun needs to be made plural before the possessive is added. Thus, for instance, the plural of Jones is **Joneses,** and the plural of Douglass is **Douglasses.** To make them possessive, simply add ', as in the **Joneses'** vacation or the **Douglasses'** cabin.)

### Another example:

You are addressing party invitations to the Weaver family and the Jones family. What do you write on the envelope?

- The **Weavers**
- The **Joneses**

Thus, you will be mailing the **Weavers'** invitation as well as the **Joneses'** invitation. Or you could say that you are mailing the **Weavers'** and the **Joneses'** invitations. If, however, someone named Weaver and someone named Jones share a residence and you are mailing only one invitation, then you are mailing the **Weaver and Jones's** invitation (to show possession of the same item by more than one person).

If Pat Jones and Chris Weaver host a party together, it's **Pat and Chris's party,** but if each one has a party, then it's **Pat's and Chris's parties.**

## Contractions

Use an apostrophe where you remove letters to show contraction:

| | | | |
|---|---|---|---|
| do n<u>o</u>t | → don't | government | → gov't |
| could <u>have</u> | → could've (not could of!) | continued | → cont'd |
| he <u>will</u> | → he'll | it <u>is</u> | → it's* |
| can<u>not</u> | → can't | who <u>is</u> | → who's* |

> *It's* is the contraction of *it is. Its* shows possession, like *my, your,* and *their. Who's* is the contraction of *who is* while *whose* is a possessive form (as in "Whose socks are on the floor?").

# Capitalization

Capitalization is a part of English grammar that dictates the appropriate use of proper nouns (i.e., names, places, and things) and adjectives as well as the beginning of a new sentence. The following explanations acquaint you with the do's and don'ts of capitalization.

- Capitalize the first letter of the first word in a sentence.

  *The sessions for the conferences are to be held inside.*

- Capitalize the first letter after a colon if it is used to begin a subtitle in a literary citation.

  *Student to student: A new form of communication (book title)*

  *Anderson, C. E. & Whittfield, J. (1999). Psychological terms: A new form of communication (1st ed.). Boston: Allyn and Bacon. (book reference)*

- Capitalize the first letter of a proper noun that is hyphenated.

  *Ellen Cole-Thomas (proper noun)*

- Capitalize other hyphenated words only when they begin a sentence.

  *Mothers-in-law are helpful in acquiring family histories.*

- Capitalize proper nouns and adjectives, including proper names and derivatives of proper names, abbreviations of names, brand names, holidays, historical events, days of the week, months of the year, street names, cities and states, monuments, drug trade names, and geographical locations.
- Capitalize the first letter of titles of dignitaries, political offices, and ethnic groups, and religions when used in specific situations to designate specific individuals.

  *The President of the United States is Bill Clayton.*

  *The Catholic Congress will meet in Kansas City, Mo.*

  *The members of the new firm are Latinos.*

  *Dean Edwards from the Department of Medicine at the University of California will be the guest lecturer for new interns at the Blackburn Eye Clinic.*

## Commas

Use commas to

- Separate items in a list
- Separate coordinate adjectives
- Join independent clauses with a coordinate conjunction (*and, but, for, or, so, yet, nor*)
- Set off introductory words, phrases, and clauses
- Set off transitional elements and tag questions
- Set off nonessential information
- Separate quoted words from words of introduction or explanation

In addition, commas have specific uses in addresses, dates, names, numbers, and correspondence.

## *Items in a List*

The items can be individual words, phrases, or clauses, but they must be all the same type, or parallel in structure, and there need not always be a conjunction. (When the items in the list already contain commas, use semicolons to separate the items—see the section on semicolons.)

Words
- red, white, and yellow
- green, orange, blue
- slowly, methodically, and deliberately
- quickly, easily, perfectly
- ran, jumped, and slid
- sat, cried, sniffed
- dog, cat, and fish
- Pat, Terry, Chris

Phrases
- Chris went to *the store, the library, and the pool.*
- Marty took many items: *my book, her pencil, Pat's markers.*
- I have looked *on the table, under the bed, and in the den.*
- Pat believes in *thinking quickly, acting spontaneously, and enjoying completely.*
- While you *watch television, chew gum, and fold laundry,* I will prepare dinner.

Clauses
- Because *it's late, the weather is awful, and I am out of gas,* I'm staying home.

## *Coordinate Adjectives*

Coordinate adjectives are those modifying words that carry equal weight when describing a noun. To check whether to use a comma, add *and* between them or reverse the order. If either works, use a comma between them.

- *the happy little boy*
- *the little happy boy* (yes)
- *the happy and little boy* (yes)

- the happy, little boy (add comma)
- *two old books*
- *old two books* (no)
- *two and old books* (no)
- two old books (no comma)
- *the charming witty professor*
- *the witty charming professor* (yes)
- *the charming and witty professor* (yes)
- the charming, witty professor (add comma)
- *many dear friends*
- *dear many friends* (no)
- *many and dear friends* (no)
- many dear friends (no comma)

## Independent Clauses

Use a comma before a coordinate conjunction (*and, but, for, or, so, yet, nor*) to join independent clauses (complete sentences). If one of the clauses is not independent, then do not use a comma with the conjunction.

*Tom caught two fish. He ate one for dinner.*

- Tom caught two fish, and he ate one for dinner.
- Tom caught two fish and ate one for dinner.

*George was hungry. He ate Tom's other fish.*

- George was hungry, so he ate Tom's other fish.

*The dog chased the ball. It rolled under the chair.*

- The dog chased the ball, and it rolled under the chair.

*I am tired. I have work to finish.*

- I am tired, but I have work to finish.
- I am tired but have work to finish.

*She had a headache. She took a nap.*

- She had a headache, so she took a nap.

*Jane did not like tonight's movie. She also didn't like the one we saw last week.*

- Jane did not like tonight's movie, nor did she like the one we saw last week.
- Jane did not like tonight's movie nor the one we saw last week.

## Introductory Words, Phrases, and Clauses

Use a comma after introductory elements.

Words
- *However,* he wanted a new gold fish.
- *Consequently,* his parents bought him a fish.
- *Tomorrow,* he will buy a second fish.
- *Obviously,* he loves fish.

Phrases
- *Early in the novel,* the author introduces the main characters.
- *In the first chapter,* we meet Mitzi.
- *Of all my cats,* Mutsy is my favorite.
- *To let me know she's hungry,* she pushes her bowl to me.
- *Sleeping on my feet,* Mutsy always knows when I awaken.

Clauses
- *When the children went to school,* their parents celebrated.
- *While the dog barked,* the rabbit ran away.
- *Because ice covered the streets,* classes were cancelled.
- *As I was telling you,* the store on the corner is having a sale.
- *Although it is raining,* we will still have the picnic.

# Semicolons and Colons

There are two reasons to use **semicolons:**

1. To join closely related independent clauses
2. To separate items containing commas in a list

## Joining Independent Clauses

Independent clauses (IC) are complete sentences. A comma does not have enough strength to join independent clauses without the help of a coordinate conjunction (*and, or, for, but, so, yet, nor*), but a semicolon wields enough power to accomplish the task. Thus, on either side of a semicolon must be an independent clause: **IC; IC.**

**Examples of joined sentences:**
*John studied many hours for the test. He had the highest score in the class.*

- John studied many hours for the test; he had the highest score in the class.
- John studied many hours for the test, and he had the highest score in the class.
- John studied many hours for the test and had the highest score in the class.

*The rains came. The river overflowed its bank.*

- The rains came; the river overflowed its bank.
- The rains came, and the river overflowed its bank.
- When the rains came, the river overflowed its bank.

## Separating Items in a List

Occasionally, items in a list already contain commas, so it becomes confusing to separate those items with more commas. Semicolons replace the commas that would normally be used to separate the listed items.

**Example:**
The guest list included Jane Doe, the club president, Fred Smith, the vice president, Pat Jones, the treasurer, and Chris Wilson, the secretary.

While it is intuitively clear that only four people are actually listed, the punctuation identifies seven: (1) Jane Doe, (2) the club president, (3) Fred Smith, (4) the vice president, (5) Pat Jones, (6) the treasurer, and (7) Chris Wilson, the secretary. To cut the guest list almost in half, use semicolons:

The guest list included Jane Doe, club president; Fred Smith, vice president; Pat Jones, treasurer; and Chris Wilson, secretary.

## Colons

Colons have some special uses including separating hours and minutes (2:00 p.m.), separating chapter and verse in Bible references (John 3:16), separating titles from subtitles (*Working Wood: A Guide for the Country Carpenter*), and concluding a salutation in a formal letter (Dear Dr. Whozit:). But if a colon is used in a sentence outside its special uses, often to signal a forthcoming list or a restatement of the point made in an independent clause, it must be preceded by an independent clause: **IC:** _____.

**Examples:**
The guest list included the following people: Jane Doe, club president; Fred Smith, vice president; Pat Jones, treasurer; and Chris Wilson, secretary. (Compare this example with the previous one. In the previous sentence, *The guest list included* is not an independent clause, so there is no colon after *included,* but in this example, *The guest list included the following people* is a complete sentence and thus requires a colon before the list.)

The child stayed awake all night waiting for one person: Santa Claus. (Compare with "The child stayed awake all night waiting for Santa Claus.")

Her backpack contained all the essential items: books, pencils, and scantrons. (Compare with "Her backpack contained books, pencils, and scantrons.")

*Moby-Dick* begins with the following words: "Call me Ishmael." (Compare with "*Moby-Dick* begins with 'Call me Ishmael.' ")

# Verbs

All actions take place in the past, the present, or the future, and verbs are the words that express the action within a sentence; they change their form to accommodate tense and number. Most verbs typically change from present to past tense by ending the verb in *-ed*. Many words require helping verbs to clarify action (e.g., forms of *to be* and *to have* "help" the main verbs in sentences).

> **Example**
> She jumps on the bed. *(present)*
>
> I jumped on the bed to play with the dog. *(past)*
>
> Andraya will jump on the bed when the dog barks. *(future)*

## *Helping Verbs*

Helping verbs are used to change verb tense. Some helping verbs are forms of *to be* and *to have* as well as *should, could, would, may, might,* and *must.*

## *Irregular Verbs*

These verbs change their spelling when used in the past tense, and helpers are needed to express the correct meaning within a sentence. Here is a list of some irregular verbs.

| *Present* | *Past* | *Past with Helpers* |
| --- | --- | --- |
| begin | began | have begun |
| break | broke | have broken |
| choose | chose | have chosen |
| drive | drove | have driven |
| eat | ate | have eaten |
| fall | fallen | have fallen |
| grow | grew | have grown |
| know | knew | have known |

| leave | left | have left |
| lie | lay | have lain |
| lay | laid | have laid |
| sit | sat | have sat |
| speak | spoke | have spoken |
| take | took | have taken |
| throw | threw | have thrown |
| write | wrote | have written |

## *Agreement Extras*

- Singular subjects are used with singular forms of verbs; plural subjects are used with plural forms of verbs. The verb *to be* is the exception.
- The pronoun *you* is always considered plural.
- The simple past form of an irregular verb should never be used with a helper.
- The past form of a verb with a helper needs a helper to be considered as a verb.
- A verb must agree with its subject, not with a noun or pronoun that comes between the subject and the verb.

# Bibliography

Anderson, C. E., Carrell, A. T., & Widdifield, J. L., Jr. (2004). *APA and MLA writing formats*. Boston: Pearson Education, Inc.

American Psychological Association. (2001). *Publication manual of the American Psychological Association* (5th ed.). Washington, DC: Author.

American Psychological Association. (1994). *Publication manual of the American Psychological Association* (4th ed.). Washington, DC: Author.

Blumenthal, J. C., Zahner, L., Frank, R., & Lazarus, A. (1966). *The English language*. New York: Harcourt, Brace.

Gibaldi, J. (1999). *MLA handbook for writers of research papers* (5th ed.). New York: MLA.

Hodges, J. C., & Whitten, M. E. (1967). *Harbrace college handbook*. New York: Harcourt, Brace.

Teall, K. M. (1971). *Black history in Oklahoma: A resource book*. Oklahoma City: Oklahoma City Public School Title III, ESEA.